I BELIEVE

It Is Fun Discovering the World Around Me, Just Like Sara, Carlo, and Teddy, the Curious Horses.

Coloring and Activity Book 9

SUZANNE MONDOUX
Illustrated by Gaëtanne Mondoux

BALBOA
PRESS
A DIVISION OF HAY HOUSE

Balboa Press books may be ordered through booksellers or by contacting:

Balboa Press
A Division of Hay House
1663 Liberty Drive
Bloomington, IN 47403
www.balboapress.com
1 (877) 407-4847

Print information available on the last page.

ISBN: 978-1-9822-2269-7 (sc)
ISBN: 978-1-9822-2270-3 (e)

Balboa Press rev. date: 02/22/2019

This book belongs to

_____

I am _____ years old

Spring had sprung on the ranch and all was green and bright. Flowers were blooming and butterflies were fluttering here and there from flower to flower and tree to tree.

The Mourning Cloak walked head downward along the oak tree trunk to feed on the dripping sap. The butterfly flapped its wings displaying its beautiful colors. The purple-black and wide bright yellow bordered the outer margins of the wings, with a row of iridescent blue spots at the inner edge radiating in the sun's rays.

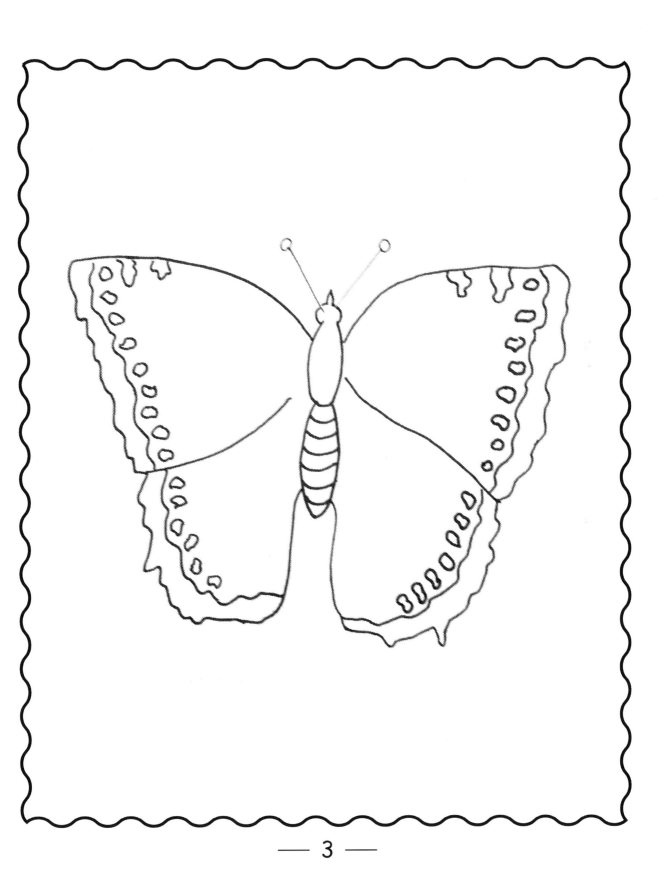

Sara the golden mare walked amongst the bright green fields surrounding the ranch. Since she left the desert where she had lived for many years with the Mustangs, Sara had become quite the explorer of her new surroundings. Jojo the dignified and respected teacher of all horses, other animals and humans set a challenge for Sara to help with the lessons on the ranch. Jojo asked Sara to decide on an expedition for the summer season.

The children and animals were excited to hear about their next lesson. They could not wait to learn where they would be going. What mysterious place would they discover? How far would they travel? It was all very exciting. They could barely stand the anticipation.

After a few days of reflection Sara had come up with an idea for the summer expedition. She called on to Carlo and Teddy for their assistance. She shared her idea with them. Teddy and Carlo thought it was brilliant.

Later that day they gathered everyone around the picnic table. Everyone huddled around the table and on top of the table. Once everyone settled Sara announced where the summer expedition would take place.

She opened the map and placed it on the center of the table. All eyes peered down at the map. The world looked up at everyone. At the far left and mid-way down, a large red irregular shape stretched east, west, north and south. "This is where we will have our summer expedition," said Sara.

She opened another map with a closer look at the location. Everyone looked down at the map, and then they looked back up at Sara.

"That is the ranch and the surrounding area," said Suzie. The girls and boys were surprised. Sophie bent forward to have a closer look at the map. Paul wiggled his way closer to examine the location, and Sam looked up at Sara with his arms crossed.

"But I thought we were going on an expedition," said Sam.

"You are," answered Sara.

Rocky reached for his guitar. "Well, at least I can bring my guitar."

Sparky the little black dog jumped up and down. He was happy to go anywhere and do anything. Sparky had grown up to become a very adventurous and inquisitive dog.

Lulu the fawn Pug sat next to him. Her two pups Bessie and Tulip, almost all grown up now, curled up at her feet.

Max the orange tabby cat was seated on Carlo's back starring down at the map. After Max had lost his family and then found them again, he returned to the ranch for the summer expedition. His family listened to his story of how he persevered and about everything he learned from Sara and the others at the ranch. They were very excited for him when he wanted to return to learn more and help others learn as well.

"This is exciting," said Max. "There will be much to explore here."

"How so?" said Sam. Sam reached for the map to have a closer look. "It is our back yard. We will not be traveling more than a day in all directions."

Sara invited Carlo and Teddy to explain to everyone why this was the ideal location for a summer expedition.

Carlo and Teddy were honored by the opportunity to share in this adventure with everyone at the ranch. They talked about how much of the world they had seen ever since they left their home. Together as friends and travel companions they dramatized the wonderful things they had seen, the amazing people and animals they met along the way, and the slew of exciting and mysterious discoveries unearthed from the four corners of the world. But what was as equally exciting and mysterious was the world that surrounded the ranch.

They walked around as they talked and talked. They pointed at the mountains. They pointed at the vast meadows all around them. They pointed at the sky. They pointed at the ground beneath their feet. They talked of all the plants, other animals, insects and everything else they could find not visible to the naked eye. There was a world to be discovered right in their back yard.

The children and animals were revved up with excitement. They could not wait to get started.

The next day everyone was ready to begin. They had gathered their gear and whatever else they needed. They had their magnifying loop, different maps with large and smaller scales. They had their notebooks and pencils, their rain gear, and tiny shovels to dig beneath the soil, and all sort of other things to help with their expedition.

That morning and for 60 more mornings they set out on a new expedition in search of treasures in their back yard.

After the 60 days the children and animals were so excited they asked if you could do the same. They would love it if you went on a 60 days expedition in your back yard or at least no more than a day trip away from your home.

This is very exciting and lots of fun. For the next 60 days get out there and discover everything you can about the different insects you find, the different plants you discover, and all the animals that you can see. Touch the rocks and feel their grit between your fingers or their smoothness after being washed over with stream water for hundreds and hundreds of years. The world is waiting for you to discover it.

Go and have some fun!!!!!

Let your imagination take you anywhere it wants to take you!

Lets begin.

Most importantly - Have fun!

Remember to smile.

Remember to laugh.

Remember to be curious and ask questions.

Remember to Believe in yourself.

Say out loud 10 times.

I Believe in myself.
I Believe in myself.
I Believe in myself.
I Believe in myself.
I Believe in myself.
I Believe in myself.
I Believe in myself.
I Believe in myself.
I Believe in myself.
I Believe in myself.

ONCE A DAY

Write about everything you discover and learn. Draw pictures of everything you see.

If you find a plant that is of interest to you, collect it and put into a plant press.

A plant press is a set of equipment used to flatten and dry plant samples so that they can be easily stored. You can find lots of different examples by searching in Google and the library on how to make your own plant press.

Your plant and flower specimens prepared in a plant press can later be glued to archival- quality card stock with their labels, and then filed in a herbarium.

I invite you to explore and discover what is:

1) Archival – quality card stock, and

2) What is an 'herbarium'?

It is very easy to make a plant press at home with newspaper and cardboard left around the house.

All you have to do is this.

1) Place a couple of pieces of newspaper on top of cardboard.

2) Place your collected plants to be pressed on top of the newspaper. Take time to position the plant as you wish for them to be pressed. Once they are dry they will be brittle.

3) Wrap a belt or string tight around the cardboard to keep the plant press flat. Place something heavy like a book on top of the plant press to keep it flat and pressed against the plants.

Now you have your own plant collection.

Remember, any time you have questions about your expedition what do you do?

That is correct!!!

You ask someone to help you.

You do your research to find the answers.

You keep asking more questions.

You continue to discover and continue to discover!

There is no end to this fun expedition!

Day 1

_____

_____

_____

_____

_____

_____

_____

_____

_____

Day 2

_____

_____

_____

_____

_____

_____

_____

_____

_____

Day 3

Day 4

_____

_____

_____

_____

_____

_____

_____

_____

_____

Day 5

_____

_____

_____

_____

_____

_____

_____

_____

_____

Day 6

_____

_____

_____

_____

_____

_____

_____

_____

_____

Day 7

Day 8

_____

_____

_____

_____

_____

_____

_____

_____

_____

Day 9

Day 10

_____

_____

_____

_____

_____

_____

_____

_____

Day 11

Day 12

_____

_____

_____

_____

_____

_____

_____

_____

_____

_____

Day 13

_____

_____

_____

_____

_____

_____

_____

_____

_____

Day 14

_____

_____

_____

_____

_____

_____

_____

_____

_____

Day 15

Day 16

_____

_____

_____

_____

_____

_____

_____

_____

_____

Day 17

_____

_____

_____

_____

_____

_____

_____

_____

_____

Day 18

_____

_____

_____

_____

_____

_____

_____

_____

_____

Day 19

Day 20

_____

_____

_____

_____

_____

_____

_____

_____

_____

Day 21

_____

_____

_____

_____

_____

_____

_____

_____

_____

Day 22

_____

_____

_____

_____

_____

_____

_____

_____

_____

Day 23

_____

_____

_____

_____

_____

_____

_____

_____

_____

Day 24

_____

_____

_____

_____

_____

_____

_____

_____

_____

_____

Day 25

Day 26

Day 27

Day 28

Day 29

_____

_____

_____

_____

_____

_____

_____

_____

_____

_____

Day 30

_____

_____

_____

_____

_____

_____

_____

_____

_____

_____

Day 31

_____

_____

_____

_____

_____

_____

_____

_____

_____

_____

Day 32

_____

_____

_____

_____

_____

_____

_____

_____

_____

Day 33

_____

_____

_____

_____

_____

_____

_____

_____

Day 34

_____

_____

_____

_____

_____

_____

_____

_____

_____

Day 35

_____

_____

_____

_____

_____

_____

_____

_____

_____

_____

Day 36

_____

_____

_____

_____

_____

_____

_____

_____

_____

Day 37

_____

_____

_____

_____

_____

_____

_____

_____

_____

Day 38

_____

_____

_____

_____

_____

_____

_____

_____

_____

_____

Day 39

Day 40

Day 41

Day 42

Day 43

_____

_____

_____

_____

_____

_____

_____

_____

_____

Day 44

_____

_____

_____

_____

_____

_____

_____

_____

_____

Day 45

Day 46

_____

_____

_____

_____

_____

_____

_____

_____

_____

_____

Day 47

_____

_____

_____

_____

_____

_____

_____

_____

_____

Day 48

Day 49

_____

_____

_____

_____

_____

_____

_____

_____

_____

Day 50

_____

_____

_____

_____

_____

_____

_____

_____

_____

_____

Day 51

_____

_____

_____

_____

_____

_____

_____

_____

_____

Day 52

_____

_____

_____

_____

_____

_____

_____

_____

_____

Day 53

Day 54

_____

_____

_____

_____

_____

_____

_____

_____

_____

Day 55

Day 56

Day 57

Day 58

Day 59

_____

_____

_____

_____

_____

_____

_____

_____

_____

Day 60

_____

_____

_____

_____

_____

_____

_____

_____

_____

WOW! YOU ARE AMAZING!!!!!!!!!!!!!!

YOU DID ALL THE FUN STUFF!

YOU PARTICIPATED IN 60 DAYS OF FUN!

KEEP GOING!

EXPLORE YOUR IMAGINATION!

BELIEVE IN YOURSELF ALWAYS!

SHARE WHAT YOU DISCOVERED AND LEARNED
ON YOUR EXPEDITION, AND THE EXPLORATION
OF YOUR IMAGINATION WITH A FRIEND!

THANK YOU FOR BEING GOOD AND KIND TO EVERY ANIMAL.

On behalf of all the ANIMALS – thank you for
making this a better world for ALL OF US!

Printed in the United States
By Bookmasters